Christopher Columbus

By Mary Dodson Wade

Consultant
Jeanne Clidas, Ph.D.
National Reading Consultant
and
Professor of Reading, SUNY Brockport

Children's Press®
A Division of Scholastic Inc.
New York   Toronto   London   Auckland   Sydney
Mexico City   New Delhi   Hong Kong
Danbury, Connecticut

Designer: Herman Adler Design
Photo Researcher: Caroline Anderson
The photo on the cover shows Christopher Columbus.

Library of Congress Cataloging-in-Publication Data

Wade, Mary Dodson.
  Christopher Columbus / by Mary Dodson Wade.
    p. cm. — (Rookie biographies)
Includes index.
Summary: Presents a brief look at the life of Christopher Columbus and
his search for a new route to the Indies.
  ISBN 0-516-22851-X (lib. bdg.) 0-516-27769-3 (pbk.)
  1. Columbus, Christopher—Juvenile literature. 2. Explorers—America—
Biography—Juvenile literature. 3. Explorers—Spain—Biography—Juvenile
literature. 4. America—Discovery and exploration—Spanish—Juvenile literature.
[1. Columbus, Christopher. 2. Explorers. 3. America—Discovery and
exploration—Spanish.] I. Title. II. Rookie biography. III. Series.
  E111 .W24 2003
  970.01'5'092—dc21

2002015138

Christopher Columbus lived more than 500 years ago. He was born in 1451 in Genoa, Italy.

Columbus loved the sea. He began sailing when he was a boy. He learned how wind and ocean currents pushed ships along.

One time, pirates sank his ship.
He grabbed an oar and swam
to land.

When he was a young man,
Columbus read a book written
by Marco Polo.

Marco Polo was an explorer.
His book told about his travels
to the Indies and the riches
he found there.

7

Marco Polo had brought back spices from his travels. The people of Europe tasted pepper, ginger, and nutmeg and wanted more.

It was a long trip over high mountains to get these spices.

Pepper

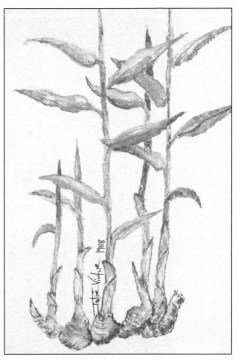

Ginger

Nutmeg

9

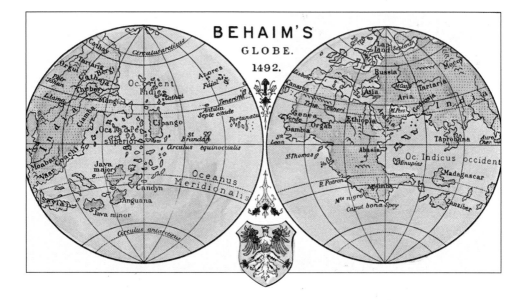

BEHAIM'S
GLOBE.
1492.

Columbus had a plan to bring spices and other treasures to Europe. His plan was to reach India, China, and Japan by going a new way.

Columbus did not want to go over the mountains. He wanted to sail west, but he did not know that land would be in his way.

Columbus needed money for his long trip. He talked to many people about his idea.

King Ferdinand and Queen
Isabella of Spain gave him
money for three ships.

In 1492, the *Santa Maria*, the *Niña*, and the *Pinta* set sail. The ships headed west.

Columbus was commander
(kuh-MAND-ur) of 90 men.
A commander tells a group of
people what to do. There were
many sailors, three doctors,
and a man who counted the
king's money.

Columbus watched the wind, the currents, and the stars.

Every day he wrote down how far the ships had sailed.

17

The sailors had never been so far from land. They became afraid. They wanted Columbus to turn back.

Columbus promised the sailors they would see land soon.

A sailor saw an island on October 12.

Columbus named the island
San Salvador and claimed the
land for Spain.

People called the Tainos lived
there. Columbus called the
native people Indians because
he thought he was in India.

Columbus sailed back to Spain.
He took six Tainos to show
the king and queen. He also
brought parrots, corn, and
chili peppers.

The king and queen made him
"Admiral of the Ocean Sea."

26

Columbus made three more trips. His son Ferdinand was on the last one. Ferdinand wrote a book about his father.

Columbus died in 1506.
He was 55 years old.
He never knew that he
had reached the Americas.

Words You Know

Christopher Columbus

ocean currents

Marco Polo

spices

King Ferdinand and
Queen Isabella

the *Santa Maria*, the *Niña*,
and the *Pinta*

San Salvador

Tainos

31

Index

About the Author

Mary Dodson Wade has written over forty books for young readers, many of them biographies. When she isn't traveling, she makes her home in Houston, Texas.

Photo Credits